Write It, Speak It
Writing a Speech They'll Applaud

© 2016 Tom Pfeifer
Managing Partner
Consistent Voice Communications, LLC
Springfield, VA

Acknowledgements

I have a lifetime of people to acknowledge and thank for making me a better writer and communicator, and thereby making this book possible. Each and every person who has touched me in some way—because you are unfortunate enough to be related to me, or you chose to be my friend, or you chose to be my enemy—has added to my growth during my journey. But I would be remiss if I did not acknowledge some particular people.

Distinguished Toastmaster Paul White, a Toastmasters' Toastmaster, suggested I write this book. He also suggested I present a workshop on speech writing. I wrote this book in preparation for the workshop.

To the rest of my Toastmasters family in GUTS (Get Up to Speak), Burgay, APS (Aspiring Professional Speakers), and friends in clubs around the world, thank you for your ongoing support and encouragement.

In addition to my relatively new speaking buddies, two writers have been supportive critics for many years.

I have known Dr. Stephanie Bluestein since she was a newspaper intern and I was her city editor at the now-defunct *Enterprise* in Simi Valley, California. She now teaches aspiring journalists their craft at California State University, Northridge. Stephanie and I have developed the habit over the years of trading manuscripts to edit. You'll find one of her pointed comments to one of my earlier works later in this book.

Tracey Lynn Shifflett and I met when we both worked on Capitol Hill. She has been a client, a friend, a confidant, and a colleague. Tracey is a freelance writer, editor, and publicist. She edited this book, so if you see any errors, blame her. I'm kidding, obviously. All errors belong to the author.

To my wife, Cathy, who had a choice but married me anyway; and to my daughters, Theresa and Clare, who had no choice in the matter; thank you for supporting me and believing in me even when I doubted myself.

Special thanks to Bob Satterthwaite and Wayne Lee. They have passed, but they were the first to give my writing a harsh critique. That much-needed kick in the butt led to a lifetime pursuit to be a better writer and communicator.

Contents

Writing is Writing 9
It's Not about You 9
Begin with a Bang 12
Keep Jargon to a Minimum 14
Structure: Outline, Mindmap, Stream of Consciousness 16
Humor and Inspiration 18
Show, Don't Tell 21
Effective Headlines 21
Rewrite, Rewrite, Rewrite 22

Speech Writing is Script Writing 25
Vocal Variety 26
Gestures 27
Staging 29
Rehearse, Rehearse, Rehearse 29

Techniques to Writing a Powerful Speech 33
The Beginning, the Middle, and the End 33
Power of Stories 35
Rhetorical Devices 36
    Power of Three 36
    Rhetorical Questions 37

  Parallelism 38
  Chiasmus 38
  Anaphora & Epistrophe 38
  Alliteration 39
  Hyperbole and Adynaton 39
Repetition, Repetition, Repetition 39
The Element of Surprise 40
Timing is Everything: Word Count to Minutes 41

And, in Closing … 43
About the Author 44
Sources 46
Appendix: Speech Sample 48
You Just WAIT Until Your Father Comes Home 48

Chapter 1:

Writing is Writing

Writing a five- to seven-minute speech is similar to writing a feature column or short story. Writing a one-hour speech is comparable to writing a short non-fiction book or novel. With few exceptions, the same rules and good practices that apply to writing for readers are applicable to writing for listeners.

We will explore exceptions in Chapter 2, but let's begin with the similarities. In this chapter we will explore why you must know your audience, how to begin with a bang, what structure to use, and much more. We begin where all good writing begins—with your audience.

It's Not about You

The first rule of all good writing is, "It's not about you. It's about them." There is a school of thought that if you write what you like, others will like it too. To a certain point I agree, because if the topic doesn't interest you, that lack of interest will come through to your audience. But writing for yourself only takes you so far. People today have the ability to target just what interests them and shut out the rest. In such a world of targeted expectations, if you want others to read your prose or come to hear you speak, you need to know what interests them. More importantly, you need to know *why* they are interested in reading your prose or coming to hear you speak. Think: "*What's in it for them?*" Because I guarantee you, they're thinking: "*What's in it for me?*"

I began my professional writing career as a journalist. My job was to accurately convey an event to those who could not be there. I can hear the anti-journalists snickering. And yes, I have read stories about a meeting I attended and wondered if the journalist was at the same meeting. But by and large, it was my job to accurately describe the meeting or event. I was my readers' eyes and ears, as most journalists try to be. As long as I focused on my readers and what was in it for them, I wrote accurate, well-rounded stories. I also tried to make the stories as entertaining and interesting as possible, but accuracy came first. That's why readers read my stories. That's what was in it for them. And because of that, I was well-respected in my community—respected enough that a Republican congressman later hired that liberal journalist as his communications director. Then, my audience became the congressman's constituents, and I wrote what was in it for them through my boss's eyes. Whether I was writing a speech, a newsletter, a press release, a tweet, or any other communication, the focus was always first and foremost on what was in it for the constituents.

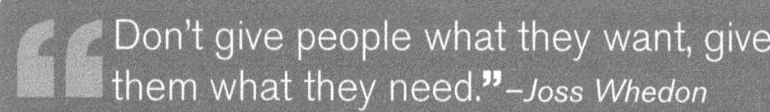

> "Don't give people what they want, give them what they need." *–Joss Whedon*

It's the same whether you are writing for a reader or a listener. Sheryl Roush, an international speaker from San Diego, broadens her reach—and income—by providing local public speaking workshops in conjunction with Toastmasters conventions. At the end of her workshops, Sheryl asks her audience for golden nuggets—the one thing each audience member will take away from the workshop and implement in his or her own public speaking repertoire.

At one workshop, my golden nugget was: It's not about you, the speaker. It's about the audience.

By then, I was not only writing speeches but delivering them. I always wrote speeches with the audience in mind, but I wasn't delivering them with the audience in mind. Now I repeat to myself before I write and before I speak: *It's about you, not me. The spotlight is on you. Not me. You're here to learn something. Or to be entertained. And I can give that to you. I want to give that to you. Because I'm a giver. And nothing makes me feel better than to give to people.*

As humans, we're wired that way, to give. It's how we evolved and survived. Without cooperation, without caring for our children and our elderly, without making sure that all made it through the winter, we would have died out as a species long ago. Scientists have found centers in the brain that are stimulated when we give. It literally makes us feel good to help others. So if you put yourself in the mindset—without getting haughty about it—that your purpose is to give to your audience, your writing will be more focused. On stage, the butterflies won't go away, but they will fly in formation.

This book is being written specifically for you—someone who wants to learn how to write more engaging, more memorable speeches from someone who has been there. That is you, isn't it?

Just as I'm thinking of you as I write this book, you need to be thinking about your audience when you write your speech. If you're in Toastmasters—and if you want to be a better speaker and you're not in Toastmasters, why aren't you?—then you'll notice many of the speech evaluation criteria includes, "Was the speech appropriate to the audience?"

This is how important knowing your audience is to writing. Novelist Kip Langello wrote nine novels that didn't sell. Then Langello created Peggy, a fictional but precise reader. Everything he wrote, he wrote for Peggy. Would she laugh here? Would this frighten her? Would she curl up with her husband at this turn of events? The next book Langello wrote sold for six figures. Peggy approved.

Here's how Langello describes Peggy:

> Before writing No. 10, I asked myself who was going to read my book. I visualized one person from that proverbial bookstore line. Not me. And not a generalization of everybody else. One person. The same way I create characters when I write, I created a reader—my ideal reader. The best fit for my book, my work. I made her a woman. Thirty-four years old. She worked in the medical records department at Jackson Memorial Hospital in Miami. Her husband worked for Orkin, spraying for termites (infestations are a big problem in Florida). She and her husband

were both big Dolphins fans and wore Dan Marino jerseys on the weekends. I made her a living, breathing person. And I gave her a name: Peggy. Then I sat down to write my novel. Every time I created a scene, I thought about Peggy reading it. Would she like this character? Was this joke going to make her laugh? Would this antagonist scare her? I Peggy-tested everything.

Why? Who is Peggy? Why is what she likes the one and only thing that will sell? Well, what she likes isn't the one and only thing that will sell. But I know Peggy's tastes inside and out, and I have learned to write for her well. **Crafting a story for Peggy forced me to use a consistent voice and style, to be consistent and focused and true to a single reader, representative of a larger niche readership. And so my novel read that way—consistent, focused, true. Not self-indulgent and occasionally meandering because I wrote it thinking only of myself, and not broad and flat because I tried to write it for the reading public at large.** (Emphasis added.)

So think about what's in it for your audience. Are they coming to hear you speak to be entertained? Are they coming to hear you speak to be informed? Are they coming to hear you speak to be inspired? What do they look like? What are they wearing? What do they do for a living? Are they happy at work? What's in it for them will dictate the form, the structure, and the tone of your speech.

Your audience isn't composed of fictional characters. They are real people. You can find out about them. Professional speakers discover all they can about the real, living, breathing people who will be in an audience before they sit down to write. Before giving workshops, at the very least, I send out a questionnaire to assess my audience's level of knowledge about the subject and discover their most burning questions. Then I can tailor my presentation to their wants, needs, and expectations. At the event, I also try to talk with the attendees before I speak and incorporate what's appropriate into my presentation.

Begin with a Bang

How many speeches have you heard start like this?

"Ladies and gentlemen, it's a pleasure to be here tonight. You all look wonderful. I'm guessing you look wonderful anyway. It's kind of hard to see you with these bright lights. Isn't the weather perfect? I'd like to thank Norman for that wonderful introduction. I hope I can live up to it."

I guarantee you won't live up to it, because my brain has already shifted to composing my grocery list. You're boring.

In 2015, the attention span of humans fell to eight seconds, according to the Statistic Brain Research Institute. That's shorter than a goldfish, which the institute pegged at nine seconds. It's also down from 2000, when humans apparently could pay attention for a full 12 seconds. Incidentally, the Institute didn't say if the goldfish's attention span rose or fell during that time.

An unsigned *iSpeakEASY* blog clocked the time to grab audience members before their minds wander at 15 seconds. That's longer than the Institute gives us credit for, but it's still not much time. You don't want to waste it. Once you lose your audience it's very difficult to get them back. So you need to begin with a bang and grab their attention right away.

Craig Valentine, the 1999 Toastmasters International World Champion of Public Speaking, believes there are three effective ways to start a speech:

- A story
- A question
- A curious statement

In a speech about telling stories, I start with telling a story. Depending on my audience and the effect I want to create, I may start with a story about four-year-olds predicting their futures, or about my first day as a newspaper intern, or even a story about my tie.

In a speech I was asked to give on "Trump, Toastmasters & 2016," I began with a question:

"Is Donald Trump succeeding because he embraces Toastmasters guidelines, or because he violates them?"

After a brief pause, I answered:

"The short answer is: 'Yes.'"

You also can combine elements to begin a speech. In a speech on how the journey to greatness never ends, I open with a curious statement followed by a question:

"I am great!" I loudly exclaim.

"How many of you have been told you were great?" Which I answer: "Most of you have, I'm sure."

These tricks of the trade work equally well with the written word. Here's the opening paragraph of a magazine article I wrote for a client:

"At Emergency Nursing 2015, a small group of emergency nurses was asked what their top three legislative issues are. While not every emergency nurse rated mental health as their top priority, everyone rated it in their top three."

That's a mini story—with a point.

I started a blog post for another client this way:

"'The journey of a thousand miles begins with a single step,' ancient Chinese philosopher Lao Tzu is widely quoted as saying.

"What if your first step is a 6,000-mile, cross-country round trip to meet with military, veterans, and their families to put faces on the suicide epidemic?"

That's a quote followed by a question.

I began another blog post—and a speech to a group of business folk—by asking:

"Do you want clients who you enjoy working with—and with whom you do your best work?"

The point is to engage your audience's brains right away.

Again, there is nothing special about speaking that demands you grab your audience immediately. It's crucial to all communication. Joshua Conran, a senior partner with brand strategy, marketing, and advertising agency Deksia, wrote in *Inc.* that advertisers have only five seconds to grab their target's attention.

Eight seconds. Fifteen seconds. Five seconds. In short, seconds count. If you want your audience to pay attention, begin with a bang, not a whimper.

You also need to end with a bang. Often, your ending is all anyone will remember. But because this chapter is about writing similarities, I'll cover ending your speech in Chapter 3.

Keep Jargon to a Minimum

At times, you may find it entirely appropriate to write a speech filled with jargon. If you're an astronomer speaking to NASA scientists, you'll most likely use a ton of scientific and NASA jargon in your speech. If you're speaking to inform the general public, however, and your topic is not necessarily familiar to your audience, you'll want to speak in simple terms. Don't be condescending, but don't use $20 words when a $5 word would do. (When I started out writing, we were warned against using a $5 word when a 50-cent word would do. Inflation.)

> "One should use common words to say uncommon things." —*Arthur Schopenhauer*

When I worked in a congressional office, I worked with many lawyers who wrote the legislation my boss would introduce. My job was to explain the legislation to the constituents and media. I did that in various ways—through print and electronic newsletters, social media, press releases, columns, and speeches. I was luckier than many congressional communicators. The lead lawyer in my office understood the need to suspend legalese when writing for the general public. But some lawyers in our office did not understand the concept of brevity. A 500-word column is not going to cover everything in the legislation. A five-minute speech is not going to cover everything in the legislation. Much of the time, you have to trust your audience to understand—unlike writing legislation where you assume it will be misinterpreted if it's not stated specifically. So I spent a great amount of my workday attempting to understand the legislation well enough to write about it coherently and concisely. To do that, I had to understand what needed to be communicated to the general public, but also what just didn't matter to them.

It goes back to who is your audience. Will they understand your technical terms? If not, define and explain them in simple terms. Don't dumb it down, just make it understandable. Do they need certain information to make an informed decision, or is it just internal processes—inside baseball—that have no real bearing on the issue? While it takes research to write coherently, your audience, in most cases, does not need to see how the sausage is made.

Structure: Outline, Mindmap, Stream of Consciousness

© Can Stock Photo Inc./dizanna

Three primary methods are used to structure a piece of writing:

- Outline
- Mind-mapping
- Stream of consciousness

I'm a big fan of stream of consciousness. I give myself a topic, then just start writing. I like to write, so I find it's the most enjoyable form for me when structuring a blog, an article, or speech. The problem with stream of consciousness writing, however, is it's the least structured structure. So once you're finished pouring ideas onto your paper, you have to rework it to give it structure. In a speech I often give, I tell a story about my tie that came out of the stream of consciousness method. The chamber of commerce I belong to decided to start a speaker's bureau. They asked me for three speech samples, and one of them I provided was "Give a Eulogy to Your Public Speaking Fears." Part of the speech centered on examples of how you could find stories anywhere. I thought: "What's the most mundane thing I could tell a story about?" I looked down at my tie and said "AHA!" Then I just started writing about my tie.

That's fine for a 500- to 800-word blog, press release, five- to seven-minute speech (which is a standard Toastmaster's speech), and sometimes even for a 30-minute speech. But for longer presentations, I write an outline first. There are points and subpoints I need to make in longer presentations, and I need a bit more structure to pull it off. For a workshop on speech writing, I wrote up an outline and sent it to Distinguished Toastmaster Paul White, one of my mentors and the person who twisted my arm to present the workshop. Paul presented me with some feedback and off I went to write the presentation. I referred to the outline from time to time, but the speech I wound up writing did not strictly follow the outline. And that's fine, as long as all the elements are in there.

I also outlined this book before I began to write it. I've shared that outline with you. It's called the Table of Contents.

I think we've all done outlines before—in school if nowhere else—but to quickly explain it, outlines have a hierarchal structure. In the case of outlining the speech writing workshop, I used four capitalized Roman numeral sections for the Introduction, Stories, Skeleton, and Structure segments. Then I used lettered subsections for the points to be made under each main section, and lowercase Roman numerals for each subpoint to be made under the subsections. All very neat and orderly.

The third method of structuring a piece of writing is mindmapping. I am not a big fan of mindmapping, perhaps because the thought of seeing where my mind goes scares the ever-loving life out of me. But it may work for you so I offer it as an alternative. Paul White is a big fan of mindmapping, which makes me wonder sometimes about Paul.

Think of mindmapping as stream-of-consciousness outlining.

Here is an excerpt from "Organizing Your Speech," one of the modules in Toastmaster International's *The Better Speaker Series*, describing mindmapping:

> A mindmap is a diagram that represents an individual's random thoughts on a particular subject. Its purpose is to discover what will be included in the speech and when it will be mentioned.
> **Step I:**
> In a mindmap, the main topic is printed in the center of the page and is circled to stand out. Ideas about how to organize a speech are recorded in squares around the main topic. The

> squares are linked to the main topic with lines. Finally, important points about those ideas are added.
>
> **Step II**:
> On a separate paper create a mindmap for one of the ideas. The idea is in the middle of the page surrounded by specific elements of that idea. For example, the specific elements related to the 'Outline' idea would be "Intro," "Body," and "Conclusion."
>
> Keep the mindmap free of clutter. Use a separate paper to record direct quotations or other extra material. Connect the extra material to the mindmap using asterisks, numbers, or color coding.

This just sounds like way too much work to me. And too much paper to mix up. But it may be the way you work best. Try it and see.

Humor and Inspiration

Toastmasters International conducts annual funny speech contests. Districts can choose between Humorous Speech or Tall Tale contests. Obviously, Humorous and Tall Tale speeches must be funny to win. The organization also conducts an annual International Speech Contest. The rules to that contest are simple. An International Speech must be between five and seven minutes long, it must be "substantially original," and it must be on a topic chosen by the speaker. That's it. There is no requirement that the speech be humorous or inspirational. But as every Toastmaster quickly learns, if it's not humorous _and_ inspirational, it will not win.

There are speeches, of course, that do not lend themselves to humor. Abraham Lincoln's *Gettysburg Address* was rightfully bereft of humor. But whenever possible, add humor to your speech or any other writing. The best way to add humor is not to tell jokes, but to tell humorous, self-deprecating stories. We'll delve into that more deeply as we delve more deeply into this book. I even used a lot of humorous stories in my eulogy to my mom. All in attendance agreed she would have loved it. Gathered family and friends certainly did (though the deacon scowled at me throughout).

> **" I want to write my own eulogy, and I want to write it in Latin. It seems only fitting to read a dead language at my funeral."**
> —Jarod Kintz

Why humor? Humor makes people feel good. When they feel good, they are more likely to remember what you said. In fact, a National Center for Biotechnology Information study found humorous sentences are better remembered than non-humorous sentences. In an article titled "How laughing leads to learning," the American Psychological Association noted research suggests humor produces psychological and physiological benefits that help students learn.

A side benefit to making your audience laugh is you're making them healthier. The Mayo Clinic lists both short- and long-term benefits of laughter. Short-term effects include stimulating organs, including releasing endorphins in the brain; relieving stress; and soothing tension. Long-term effects include improving your immune system and relieving pain.

I can certainly attest to the health benefits of laughter. I credit it with getting my family through my daughter's diagnosis of cancer at the age of 19 and the ensuing treatment. It was a road through hell made lighter by the fact that none of us lost our sense of humor—led by my daughter Theresa herself.

Here is an excerpt from an email I wrote to family and friends toward the end of our ordeal:

> Wednesday morning, I packed the three suitcases, three bags of food, the rollaway cooler, a bag of blankets, two inflatable beds, two backpacks, and the wheelchair into the van, and hauled Theresa and Cathy through city traffic to the hospital. To receive doxorubicin, Theresa's platelet counts have to be at least 75,000. On Wednesday, they were at 34,000. So Cathy, Theresa, and I got back in the van and headed home, where I proceeded to unload the three suitcases, three bags of food, the rollaway cooler, a bag of blankets, two inflatable beds, two backpacks, and the wheelchair.

> Friday morning I again loaded the three suitcases, three bags of food, the rollaway cooler, a bag of blankets, two inflatable beds, two backpacks, and the wheelchair into the van, and Cathy, Theresa, and I headed back to the hospital. This time the blood test showed her platelet levels had fallen even farther, to 30,000. So they pumped a couple of bags of blood into her while I went to spend a few hours at the office. Then I went back to the hospital, picked them up, returned home and again unloaded the three suitcases, three bags of food, the rollaway cooler, a bag of blankets, two inflatable beds, two backpacks, and the wheelchair. Actually, in the spirit of full disclosure, Clare helped me unload Friday and I left the wheelchair in the van.
>
> Regardless, on this coming Tuesday, god willing and the creek don't rise, I will reload the three suitcases, three bags of food, the rollaway cooler, a bag of blankets, two inflatable beds, and two backpacks back into the van with the wheelchair and head back to the hospital. With Cathy and Theresa of course. And, god willing and the creek don't rise, Theresa's platelets will have rebounded and will have stayed rebounded and she will receive her last doxorubicin treatment.

There also are speeches that do not lend themselves to inspiration. A demonstrative speech on semiconductors, I suppose, would not need to be particularly inspirational. But whenever a speech lends itself to inspiration, use it.

An inspirational speech, as defined by Toastmasters International, motivates "an audience to improve personally, emotionally, professionally, or spiritually. It encourages listeners to experience greater success, adopt higher goals or ideals, or contribute to the goals of an organization." Inspirational speeches connect with an audience on an emotional level. Some spots in inspirational speeches will bring their audiences to tears. This is fine. Just make sure the overall tone of the speech is optimistic and encourages the audience. When you connect with an audience on an emotional level, you have them eating out of the palm of your hand.

Show, Don't Tell

If you haven't heard "Show, Don't Tell" before, you've never written anything. But even if you have, it's always good to remind. "Show, Don't Tell" means to be descriptive in your writing. As Russian physician, playwright, and author Anton Chekhov once said, "Don't tell me the moon is shining; show me the glint of light on broken glass."

Craig Valentine calls it checking the VAKS. VAKS stands for Visual, Auditory, Kinesthetic, and Smell. We all learn in different ways. Some of us are visual learners. I, for one, have a hard time remembering someone's name until I see it written down. Some of us learn best when it bounces off our eardrums. Some of us are touchy-feely—we learn by doing, by physical action. All of us with a sense of smell are smelly learners. Smell is the most potent recall sense. Mention an apple pie baking in the kitchen oven and most of us recall memories of Thanksgiving.

Like anything else, however, don't overdo it. I worked for a congressman who claimed to hate adjectives and adverbs. He wanted his speeches written in simple, declarative sentences. That's extreme on the other end, but he had heard too many descriptive-laden speeches that didn't say anything of substance, and he wasn't about to be caught in that trap. You don't want to be caught in that trap either, so don't be so descriptive that you lose the point in the process.

Effective Headlines

Headlines are used to publicize your speech, even if it's just five minutes before you jump on stage. But if you're marketing your speech ahead of time, a good headline can sell tickets. It can draw people in. Use the headline to set the stage before you hit the stage. Make it brief, punchy, and catchy enough that the audience is already anticipating what you have to say. Do not make it misleading. A friend of mine recently gave a speech titled, "Looking into the Eye of a Lion." What do you think the speech was about? I certainly didn't think it would be a speech about the Lion's Club. That would be a fine title to give a speech you were presenting to the Lion's Club, because they would have understood the twist immediately. But don't have your audience anticipating one thing, then throw them a curveball. I call that being too cute for your own good. I know, because I'm too cute a lot.

You can write the headline before you write the speech or after, but you have to write a headline that encapsulates your speech. A headline should contain 15 or fewer words. Writing a headline in 15 or fewer words does more than clue your audience in to what you're going to tell them before you tell them. From a more basic perspective, if you can't sum up your speech in 15 words or less, you need to rewrite it because it is going to be rambling and unfocused. Guaranteed. Make the headline as snappy as you can while still encapsulating your message. I always write a headline early in the speech writing process. Then I usually rewrite it one, two, sometimes three or more times as I'm revising my speech.

Rewrite, Rewrite, Rewrite

Which brings us to the most critical piece of general writing advice. Your first draft is just a draft. It's going to be horrible. You have to rewrite it. Many times.

I was riding the bus with my friend Jenn several years back, talking about our work passions. She said she admired my ability to write. To paraphrase:

"I like to write. But it never comes out well."

To which I replied with a James Michener quote:

"I'm not a very good writer, but I'm an excellent rewriter."

(Ernest Hemingway put it a lot more colorfully, as Hemingway was wont to do.)

Every professional writer I know is an excellent rewriter.

I apply three golden rules to everything I write:

1. Write, then rewrite, and, if necessary, rewrite again.
2. Print it out and read it aloud. Then rewrite.
3. Have someone with good editing skills take a look at it. If necessary, rewrite again.

Only then is a piece ready to be released to the world.

There is no rule on how many rewrites a piece should undergo. I rewrite until I'm satisfied it is the best it can be or a deadline forces me to push the send button. I've written pieces with which I was satisfied after the first rewrite. But unless I'm posting to Facebook or Twitter, that's rare. (Yes, I do edit my posts before I post. Facebook now allows you to edit after you post, and I've done that too.) For short pieces of 1,000 words or less, most of what I write goes through a minimum of three rewrites before I think I'm done. A rewrite could be as simple as tightening up some sentences. It could be as involved as moving some paragraphs around for better flow. Sometimes I've found a nut buried in the piece and rewrote it with that nut as my lead. And that doesn't count the partial rewrites I do within a piece as I'm writing it.

A recent 800-word column went through several massive rewrites. After the first draft, I realized I needed additional research. I found it and plugged it in, but it still had a hole in the flow. I did some more research and added it to the mixture. Then I moved words, sentences, and paragraphs around, deleted some now superfluous material, and massaged it until it felt and read right.

Once I thought I was finished, I printed out the piece and read it aloud. You'd be surprised how many errors you catch when you read a piece aloud. One of my old editors used to tell a story about a visiting editor walking into his newsroom. When asked if he could pick out the best writers, the visiting editor said, "Sure," and pointed to three reporters. "How did you know?" the hosting editor asked. "Because their lips are moving," he replied.

Words are meant to be spoken. I don't write with my lips moving. I'm not that coordinated. But I also don't send out anything until I've read it aloud. You'll find a lot of typos, dropped words, and flow problems when reading a piece aloud. In short, oral reading always leads to a stronger piece.

Next, I give it to someone else to read. A mentor told me eons ago that a professional writer never publishes until at least one other set of eyes have looked it over. I have twin daughters who have been editing my writing for nearly two decades. They are now 29 and still love finding the errors in their daddy's ways. If you don't have children, find someone else to edit. If the first person you pick doesn't find errors in at least two out of every three pieces you write, then find someone else. Because you *will* make errors you don't see, no matter how many times you review it. That's why God invented editors.

Writing, rewriting, reading aloud, and giving it to an editor may not make you a James Michener. But you will be prouder of your writing. Then, when someone compliments your writing skills while complaining about their own, you can smile and say: "I'm not a very good writer, either. But I'm an excellent rewriter."

Chapter 1 Callback

Here's what we discussed in Chapter 1:
- Always start with your audience in mind. Create an ideal audience member and ask, What's in it for them?
- Start strong. You literally have seconds to grab your audience's attention.
- Don't use $20 words when a $5 word will do
- Choose a structure that works best for you
- Be humorous and inspirational
- Show, Don't Tell
- Use effective headlines
- And by all means, rewrite, rewrite, rewrite

Now let's move into Chapter 2 and the specialty of speech writing.

Chapter 2

Speech Writing is Script Writing

Now that we know how similar speech writing is to any other type of writing, let's look at the differences.

As I noted earlier, read written copy aloud when rewriting because words are meant to be spoken. A speech by definition, however, is written to be spoken. It's not a passive instrument like a printed page. A speech has major advantages over the printed page, because you—the speaker—make the words come alive.

Many speechwriters just write a speech as if it were any other piece of writing. But if you want to have maximum impact, I suggest you write a script by incorporating stage directions. Because a good speech is acted out as well as spoken. But before we get to stage directions, let's discuss vocal variety and gestures.

Vocal Variety

Canadian speech coach Andrew Dlugan teaches the four P's of vocal variety: Pace, Pitch, Power, and Pauses. Here is how he describes it:

> **Pace**—One of the easiest ways to incorporate variable pace is to slow down through key statements.
>
> **Pitch**—A convenient way to hit different pitch points is to play with different emotional content. A sad voice takes on a different pitch than a content voice, which is distinct from an excited voice, and so on. Stories are good speech building blocks for many reasons, including how they bring a speaker's voice alive through different emotions.
>
> **Power** (Volume)—Don't overdo it with changes in volume. Again, align your variations in volume with emotional content. Anger or joy tends to bring out a loud voice. Fear or sadness calls for a quiet voice.
>
> **Pauses**—There are a multitude of ways to incorporate pauses in a meaningful way. For this speech, keep it straightforward. Make sure you've got short pauses following every sentence, and longer pauses at the ends of paragraphs or transitions within your speech.

I used extreme vocal variety for a humorous speech that brought me to the district finals in a Toastmasters International competition. The characters in the speech were my mom, my dad, and me. For my mom, I used a high-pitched, almost screeching voice. For my dad, I used a booming, low-pitched voice. For me as a child, I used a pitch just slightly higher than my normal voice. My narrator voice was my normal speaking voice. I used pauses throughout. I used three stories in the speech and separated them by long pauses. I used shorter pauses to set up scenes within the stories. I slowed down and sped up.

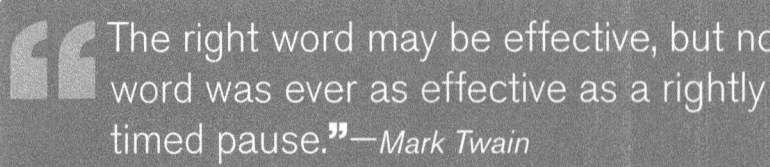

> The right word may be effective, but no word was ever as effective as a rightly timed pause." —*Mark Twain*

If there is a standard way to notate vocal variety when writing a speech, I haven't found it. However, there are various ways you can notate vocal variety when writing your speech. CAPS for loud voices. Em dashes for long pauses, hyphens for shorter pauses. Italics for when you want to slow down and emphasize a sentence. A combination of underlining and caps to indicate a particular emphasis on a word or phrase within a sentence to be spoken loudly. If you're writing a speech for yourself, use whatever works for you. If you're writing for others, agree on a format that works for you both. Many speechwriters don't notate vocal variety in the written speech at all. I suggest, however, that you do find a way to notate it—especially if you're a novice speaker.

Here's how the opening of my humorous speech would look with vocal variety notated.

You Just WAIT Until Your Father Gets Home! *[Indicates it's very loud, with "WAIT" as the accented word]*

Mr. Contest Master, Fellow Toastmasters, Most Distinguished Guests, *[Indicates normal voice]*

Yes – I – was - that - kid. *[Indicates normal voice level with pauses between every word, with a slightly longer pause between "Yes" and "I" and emphasis on "Yes" and "that"]*

Gestures

Gestures also differentiate speech writing from other types of writing.

Toastmasters International, in its manual *Gestures: Your Body Speaks*, categorizes gestures as descriptive, emphatic, suggestive, and prompting. Descriptive gestures clarify or enhance a verbal message. Use them to indicate size, movement, or location. An emphatic gesture adds emphasis. Slapping my hand to suggest my mother's wooden spoon is an emphatic gesture. Use suggestive gestures to indicate emotions or ideas. A shrug of the shoulder is a suggestive gesture. Prompting gestures are those you wish your audience to mimic—raising your hand, clapping, or standing up and cheering.

Have you ever heard the admonition that more than half of communication is nonverbal? Toastmasters International makes that claim in its *Gestures* manual. That admonition comes from research conducted in the 1960s by Albert Mehrabian. He deduced that communication was 55 percent body language, 38 percent vocal variety, and a mere 7 percent the words we speak. I have always been skeptical of those numbers because body language can be misread in so many ways. For example, I like to fold my arms across my chest. Just about everyone says folding your arms across your chest is a sign of resistance and closed-mindedness. But I'm often listening intently when I do it. It's just a comfortable position for me.

In a *Psychology Today* article, Jeff Thompson, PhD, warns against putting too much faith in an absolute formula. The percentage is situational, he writes, and should not be taken as accurate in every situation.

Having said that, if you're on stage giving a speech, even if you're talking about pea soup, your gestures will have great impact on your audience. They will have great impact on you too, because physical movement lessens nervousness. Your stomach may be doing the jig before you hit the stage but as soon as you make your first purposeful gesture, the nervousness should melt away.

In the humorous speech I described above, I used hand slaps repeatedly throughout the speech—palm-to-back-of-hand for a wooden spoon and palm-to-palm for my mom's flip-flops slapping against her heals. I stretched my right arm high above my head to indicate my father's height and my left arm to my shoulder to indicate my mother's shortness. I acted out digging a hole and lighting a fire. I'm not much for writing gestures into a script, but you may consider it. I find that if I'm saying, "I was digging, and digging, and digging," then I'm going to act it out. However, if gestures don't come easy to you, read your script and look for places where gestures may be used and note them in brackets. Example:

I was digging, and digging, and digging. *[Simulate digging with a shovel]*

Make sure your gestures are purposeful, they add to your dialogue, and they come off as natural. Use them to punctuate your speech. A fellow Toastmaster told a gripping story about his uncle on the Bataan Death March during World War II. In his first telling, he startled the audience—and grabbed their attention—by yelling, "Get up!" But he told the rest of the story with very little movement or vocal variety from center stage. It's a story that screams for gestures and stage movement. When he incorporates those, as I'm sure he will, he will have a great speech.

Other gestures are done with the entire body. Step forward to indicate you're making an important point. Step back to indicate you've completed an important point. You also can step back to indicate fear at a fearful point in your story. Facial expressions also fall under gesturing. Smile and the world—and your audience—smiles with you. Pout. Squint. Open your eyes and your mouth. Allow tears to roll down your cheeks. Your audience will get it. And they'll be one with you.

Staging

This is where a written speech most resembles a script. Add stage directions. Your speech has order. Your staging must have order too. If you're telling your speech in chronological order, you may start at one end of the stage and work yourself across as you move through time. If your speech jumps between childhood, your teenage years, and adulthood, establish a point on the stage for each of those periods and return to that part of the stage—or, at the very least, gesture toward it—each time you speak about that time in your life. My humorous speech was location specific. The events took place in my backyard, the driveway and garage, and the kitchen. My notations in the script looked like this:

[Stage Center: Kitchen]
[Stage Left: Backyard]
[Stage Right: Driveway/Garage]

Those notations preceded the dialogue for each story and, at times, within the story.

Other stage directions may include the use of props—where they are before you use them, when you use them, or what you do with them after you've used them. If you are having a panel discussion, stage directions may include where the lectern is relative to the panelists, the seating arrangement for the panelists, whether or not they are speaking from their seats or moving to the lectern. See the addendum for how my humorous speech is laid out.

Toastmasters speeches are always given from the stage. But professional speakers walk among their audiences at the appropriate time to give the audience an enhanced feeling of connectedness.

Rehearse, Rehearse, Rehearse

The Rehearse, Rehearse, Rehearse strategy follows the Rewrite, Rewrite, Rewrite strategy of all writing, except you are performing and rewriting based on what works and what doesn't. As for practicing opportunities, I know of no better organization than Toastmasters. For 15 years I worked on Capitol Hill and wrote speeches for politicians, but I did not give them myself because I was terrified to speak in front of audiences. Then I joined Toastmasters. Now I grab every available speaking opportunity. Toastmasters offers a nurturing atmosphere to practice the craft of public speaking. You receive noncritical feedback from your fellow Toastmasters on what you have done well and suggestions on ways you can improve. I suggest joining a club that meets at least twice a month. My home club meets every week. That gives me ample opportunities to rehearse, rehearse, rehearse.

Toastmasters is relatively inexpensive. Club dues are $36 every six months, although some clubs tack on a few extra dollars to pay for meeting space and equipment. (Dues will rise to $45 every six months in October 2016.) Still, in most cases, for less than $100 a year, you can get some of the best public speaking training available.

Before I speak or present workshops before a business or civic organization, I first try out my speech on my fellow Toastmasters. The feedback allows me to tweak my presentations before I present them to the public. In at least one case, I completely reworked the presentation after first presenting it to my Toastmasters club. The subject was core messaging for small businesses. I threw a quick speech together based on a blog I had written. Because I was giving the speech before a business networking group in less than a week, I requested pointed feedback. Because I'm now an accomplished Toastmaster, it's acceptable to weigh comments more heavily on ways I can improve, rather than on what worked. I received what I asked for. It did not flow correctly. I did not lay out in the beginning my goals for the presentation. I had a clear opening, body, and closing, but the closing was weak. I tried some new presentation techniques that fell flat. Based on the feedback, I completely reworked the presentation, wowed my business audience, and picked up a contract.

For the humorous speech contest, I practiced the speech before five different Toastmasters clubs in the two weeks between the third round and the final competition. I enlisted 2013 District 27 Humorous Speech Champion Arti Kumari to coach me on staging techniques. I practiced the speech at least once a day. I took the feedback from the clubs and Arti and I tweaked it repeatedly. Though I didn't win, I know it was the most powerful speech I have given in a competition to date. If you are a member of Toastmasters—and again if you are not, I urge you to do so—compete in contests. They will make you a better speechwriter and a stronger presenter.

Remember, you're writing a script. Act out your speech and incorporate stage directions and vocal inflections in your written speech to direct you. And, rewrite it until it feels right.

Chapter 2 Callback

Speech writing is writing for the eyes and ears. For that you need:
- The four P's of vocal variety: Pace, Pitch, Power, and Pauses
- Descriptive, emphatic, suggestive, and prompting gestures
- Order by incorporating stage directions
- And, by all means, rehearse, rehearse, rehearse

Now let's add some spice to your writing.

Chapter 3

Techniques to Writing a Powerful Speech

We've discussed ways in which all writing is similar. We've discussed how speech writing is more akin to script writing. This chapter provides you with techniques to writing better, more powerful speeches through storytelling, using the Power of Three and other rhetorical devices, and timing. But let's begin at the beginning.

The Beginning, the Middle, and the End

As I mentioned earlier in this book, your opening has to draw in your audience. The body of your speech gives them the meat. Your ending needs to be as strong as your beginning and leave your audience with something memorable. The easiest and most basic structure is to tell them what you're going to tell them, tell them, then tell them what you told them.

We covered the opening extensively in Chapter 1 under the heading "Begin with a Bang." When beginning your speech with a bang, make sure your opening relates to the rest of your speech. Otherwise, you'll only confuse your audience and they'll never want to listen to you again. If fact, it's doubtful they'll listen to your whole speech anyway. Where *did* I put my grocery list?

Your opening also should lay out the journey ahead for you and your audience. That's the "tell them what you're going to tell them" component.

The second most important part of a speech is the ending. You have to end as strong as you opened—perhaps stronger—or your audience will walk away feeling empty. It is the last impression you will leave with your audience and is often the only thing they will remember. "Wait!" you're saying. "I just spoke for an hour and the end may be the only thing they remember?" Yup. So make it memorable. You came in with a bang; go out with a bang. You're going to tell them what you told at the end, but it shouldn't be the last thing you tell them. Like your opening, it can be a story, a quote, or a joke. Just make sure your ending neatly ties up the themes of your speech.

You may be asking, "What about the ask?" The ask—or call to action—can come toward the end of your speech, but it should never be the end. Remember, your speech is for your audience. Smoothly work in the ask or call to action at the appropriate part of your speech. The end is rarely—if ever—the appropriate part.

Craig Valentine offers three tips to closing a speech. One is simply to signal that you're closing. That wakes up the people whose minds have wandered off— because your audience is not going to hang on to your every word, no matter how good you are. Letting them know you're about to wrap up will either have them saying to themselves, "Thank God," or they'll realize you're about to say something important they should pay attention to.

Valentine's second tip is to call back to your main points and anything else you want your audience to remember. That's the "tell them what you told them" aspect of the closing.

Valentine's final tip is to end with a bang, just as you opened with a bang. The bang does not have to be loud in a vocal variety sense, but it must have impact on your audience. Valentine suggests closing with an impactful story that adds punch to all you've said before. Which is a perfect segue into the Power of Stories.

Power of Stories

Why stories? For two reasons.

One, people relate to stories much more than they do numbers or a recitation of facts. We're humans. We've been telling stories around the fire since we could first utter words. Think about all the family stories you've heard that have been passed down from generation to generation. We relate to stories—and the storyteller—and are much more likely to remember what he or she said, as well as comprehend it. But here's the kicker for you as someone trying to eulogize your fears: stories are easier for the speaker to remember too.

When I first embarked on the road to public speaking, I tried to memorize my speeches. I failed completely. My brain would freeze on stage. I was dying up there. My friend and mentor Paul White mentioned one day that he, too, tried memorization and it didn't work for him either. So then he tried just telling stories, and he could do that. So I tried telling stories too. And it worked.

Listeners remember stories too. It's a win-win. In fact, scientists tell us stories activate the brain. Archeologists tell us storytelling has been around at least as long as cave paintings, and probably longer. Advertisers use them to sell to us. Comedians use them to make us laugh. Speakers use them to make their speeches memorable.

So what makes a great story? First, it must be relatable. You and I must connect emotionally. One of the stories I tell is about my first day working in a newspaper office. I had been told by my college journalism professor at the end of my freshman year—my freshman year—that as far as she was concerned, I was already a professional and there wasn't much more she could teach me. That certainly swelled my ego. The copy editor who crumpled up my first story and threw it in my face, growling, "Rewrite that. I can't turn this into the proofreader," popped my ego like a pricked balloon.

It's a story of puffed up failure and lessons learned. And most everyone can relate to that.

A key ingredient of a great speech is to spark action. I have several stories that appear in different speeches. The story I tell about my first day working at a newspaper; stories about my mom, dad, and siblings—even the story about my tie. They're all stories I've used in speeches multiple times. The key is to use them to make the point you want to make. And the same stories can be used to make different points.

> "Ideas are like rabbits. You get a couple and learn how to handle them, and pretty soon you have a dozen." —*John Steinbeck*

So, you now know stories can come from anywhere: a church outing, perhaps; maybe a conversation around the dinner table. Your childhood. Your working life. Your parents. Your kids. You also know why telling stories in speeches are important: Because you remember them! And so does your audience! Stories provide an emotional bond between you and your audience.

So what are you going to do to remember your speeches and make them memorable? Tell stories!

Rhetorical Devices

The following are some of the more common rhetorical devices used in speech writing, but not necessarily the most common. Not listed here, for example, are metaphors, similes, or idioms. (The aforementioned Arti Kumari gives a great speech on idioms. She hails from India and when she arrived in the United States she was told to hold her horses. She looked around and didn't see any horses to hold onto, though it was raining cats and dogs.) For that reason, this is not a complete, nor even, a comprehensive list. Some English scholars spend a lifetime studying and analyzing rhetorical devices. If this piques your interest, search "rhetorical devices" and feast on a menu of rhetorical choices.

Power of Three

My mother used to say if you ask a child at the age of four what he or she wants to be when he or she grows up, what the child says is what the child will become. My brother Michael told my mom at the age of four that he was going to be a lawyer. He is a lawyer. I told my mom at the age of four that I was going to be a writer. I am a writer. My brother Larry told my mother at the age of four that he was going to be singer. He's a custodial engineer.

Comedians know the Power of Three: two to set up the joke by setting expectations and the third for the punch line. Why three? Just as humans are wired to tell and remember stories, humans are wired to remember things in threes. A speech has an opening, a body, and a closing. Tell what you're going to tell them, tell them, then tell them what you told them. This book has three chapters.

A couple of university professors published a scholarly paper in 2013 titled, *When Three Charms but Four Alarms: Identifying the Optimal Number of Claims in Persuasion Settings*. Their studies showed three was the optimal number when trying to persuade. In a series of experiments, the duo found subjects became skeptical of marketers' claims when the series of claims hit four.

A fellow political consultant and I argued one time when I insisted the candidate we worked with weave three points into any speech she gave. Not two. Not four. But three. The fellow writer insisted that wasn't necessary because many great speeches used other speech techniques and did not use the Power of Three. He specifically pointed to President John Kennedy's Inaugural Address as an example. It was written by Ted Sorenson, one of the great speechwriters of all time. So I showed my fellow writer all the places in the speech that used the Power of Three. Look at it. It's there. Yes, Sorenson incorporated many rhetorical devices. The Power of Three was one of them. He used it because the Power of Three is a very basic rhetorical device—not just in speech writing but in writing in general—and one that will serve you well.

Rhetorical Questions

A rhetorical question is one you ask without expecting an answer. Politicians in particular are adept at the rhetorical question.

"Can anyone look at the record of this Administration and say, 'Well done'?"—presidential candidate Ronald Reagan, 1980.

"Do you want to see the flower of the manhood of this country which has brought everlasting glory to our nation neglected in the hour of its greatest need and afraid to face temptation?"—John D. Rockefeller, Jr.

"Now, I know many Republicans have sworn an oath never to raise taxes as long as they live. How can it be that the only time there's a catch is when it comes to raising taxes on middle class families? How can you fight tooth and nail to protect high-end tax breaks for the wealthiest Americans, and yet barely lift a finger to prevent taxes going up for 160 million Americans who really need the help? It doesn't make sense."—President Barak Obama, 2011

I gave you examples of rhetorical questions from my own works in Chapter 1:

"Is Donald Trump succeeding because he embraces Toastmasters guidelines, or because he violates them?"

"How many of you have been told you were great?"

"What if your first step is a 6,000-mile, cross-country round trip to meet with military, veterans, and their families to put faces on the suicide epidemic?"

Are you going to use rhetorical questions?

Parallelism

Parallelism is a broad rhetorical category under which many of the other rhetorical devices fall. It is merely repetition of measures, beats, or words that lend themselves to a rhythmic sentence structure. An example would come from John F. Kennedy's 1963 Inaugural Address when he said, "we shall pay any price, bear any burden, meet any hardship, support any friend, oppose any foe …" Another would be Abraham Lincoln's epistrophe in his *Gettysburg Address*: "of the people, by the people, and for the people."

Chiasmus

Aside from being the coolest word for a rhetorical device, it's a pretty cool device. Chiasmus comes from the Greek word for crossing, and the device basically crosses itself in a sentence when two or more otherwise parallel clauses reverse themselves. The most famous example of chiasmus again comes from JFK's Inaugural Address, in which he proclaims, "Ask not what your country can do for you, ask what you can do for your country."

Anaphora & Epistrophe

Anaphora is repetition of a word or phrase at the beginning of a sentence. Epistrophe is repetition of a word or phrase at the end of a sentence.

A perfect example of anaphora is Martin Luther King Jr.'s 1963 *I Have a Dream* speech, in which eight successive paragraphs began with the words, "I have a dream."

Two years later, President Lyndon Johnson provided us with this memorable epistrophe in his *Voting Rights Act Address*: "There is no Negro problem. There is no Southern problem. There is no Northern problem. There is only an American problem."

Alliteration

Alliteration is a very common rhetorical device. It's also one of my favorites, particularly for titles. Alliteration is repetition of the initial letter or sound in a series of words. I titled the blog I wrote after I didn't place in the humorous speech contest finals, *Lessons Learned from Losing*. I titled another speech *Message Manipulation Made Easy*. The subtitle in this book, Begin with a Bang, was originally Start with a Bang. I changed it for alliterative effect. But alliteration is not only for titles. We all know "Peter Piper picked a peck of pickled peppers." *Rowan & Martin's Laugh-In* aficionados will remember "the flying, fickle finger of fate."

Hyperbole and Adynaton

Hyperbole is exaggeration. "He was as big as a house." In a speech titled, *Triple C's: Clear, Concise and Consistent*, I asked, "Have you ever read something that went on and on and found yourself nodding off, your head bouncing like a Bryce Harper bobblehead doll?" Adynaton is hyperbole taken to its impossible extreme. "When pigs fly." "When hell freezes over." I'm not smart enough to invent an adynaton.

Repetition, Repetition, Repetition

We've discussed Rewrite, Rewrite, Rewrite. We've discussed Rehearse, Rehearse, Rehearse. Now let's discuss repetition as a writing device.

I used repetition a lot in my humorous speech. Every kitchen scene was repeated nearly verbatim until the very last moments of the very last scene. My mother's flip-flops slapping against her heels was a recurring image. Her slapping her hand with the wooden spoon happened repeatedly. My father telling me to, "Stand up, son!" occurred twice.

Look back at the email I wrote toward the end of my daughter's cancer treatments and the descriptive repetition of loading and unloading the van.

But repetition has other uses beyond setting up a humorous scene. It's a memory device for your audience. There is a great debate about how many times someone needs to hear your message before it sinks in. Marketers generally follow the Rule of Seven, but many claim that to be hogwash. Regardless of the precise number, everyone agrees that repetition is necessary for people to grasp your message. That's the thinking behind the "tell them what you're going to tell them, tell them, then tell them what you told them" strategy.

Ryan Avery used repetition very effectively in his 2012 Toastmasters International World Championship speech, *Trust Is a Must*. In it, he tells stories about growing up and getting in trouble, about being ripped off, and about getting married. That phrase was repeated throughout his speech, as was the word "trust" itself. I'm in the process of writing my next contest speech, tentatively titled *Laughter Is Contagious* about my daughter's battle with cancer. You can be sure that line—or another—will be repeated throughout the speech. Like in Avery's speech, make it part of your stories, not just a line you drop so often.

Craig Valentine uses what he refers to as callbacks in his speeches. One way of using callbacks is to call back to your previous point or points before moving onto the next one. That, too, is a form of repetition that assists your audience in remembering your key points. I use callbacks at the end of each chapter to review the key points. But that's not all. Refer to the beginning of this chapter and the beginning of Chapter 2. You'll find I also called back to the previous chapter's primary message before I introduced you to the next concept. At the beginning of this chapter, I also call back briefly to the concepts raised in Chapters 1 and 2.

Use repetition to set up a humorous scene, to hammer your primary message home, and to assist your audience in remembering your key points.

The Element of Surprise

Surprise spices up a speech. It can be used to create humor, such as my story about my mom and four-year-olds. It's also a wonderful way to open and close a speech. My mother screeching "You just wait until your father comes home" at the opening of my humorous speech certainly surprised people who heard it for the first time. I opened a speech about greatness being a journey, not a destination, by declaring, "I'm great!" which also was effective. My humorous speech ends with a surprise built on the same concept as my mom and four-year-olds story. I set expectations by telling two stories that ended similarly, then ended the third story with a twist. You also can build in surprises within your speech. Have you ever watched a speaker with a PowerPoint presentation? In a speech on core messaging, I turned off the PowerPoint about midway through and read passages from two books. I then turned the PowerPoint back on to complete my speech. It was surprising enough that it was mentioned by the audience during the comments section of the meeting. You can also have the audience do a small activity during the speech, which brings its own surprises.

Think of ways to build surprises into your speech for a more rewarding experience—for you and your audience.

Timing is Everything: Word Count to Minutes

> "To talk well and eloquently is a very great art, but that an equally great one is to know the right moment to stop."
> —Wolfgang Amadeus Mozart

When I worked on Capitol Hill, one of the weekly newspapers the congressman liked to submit columns to had a strict 500-word policy. If you submitted a column that counted out to 501 words, it was rejected. One day, the editor called me and said, "That's unbelievable. This is the third column you've submitted in a row at exactly 500 words. How do you do it?"

Remember the section on Rewrite, Rewrite, Rewrite? That's how it's done. Turning clauses into adjectives. Taking out superfluous terms. Making a point simpler. I had to put 50 pounds of ideas my boss had on a position and fit it into a five-pound sack. Making them both happy was my job.

When you speak to an audience, you're allotted a certain amount of time to speak. It could be 10 minutes. It could be an hour. You may be giving a three-hour presentation. Never go over your allotted time. In fact, for best practices, end it with time to spare. If you give a powerful presentation and let your audience go a little early, they will praise you that much more for giving them "free time." If however, you give a powerful presentation and go over time, you may just squander your powerful presentation. Your audience is composed of very busy people. If they start checking the time on their cellphones or watches because you're holding them hostage, your reviews are going to be far lower.

After you write your speech, time yourself as you rehearse. Forget written-words-per-minute. Everyone speaks at a different pace. Leave time for laughter, questions, or any number of interruptions. Know ahead of time what you're going to cut from your presentation if you go long. And, when giving a speech, be conscious of the time, either by tracking it yourself or by having someone signal you at predetermined intervals.

Be the one who surprises everyone by consistently packing 50 pounds into a five-pound sack and you'll be in great demand.

If you incorporate many of these techniques in your speech, you will give a more powerful presentation. Start by incorporating stories and the Power of Three. Give a powerful beginning and closing. And make sure you time yourself as you rehearse.

Now it's time to close out this book. But first:

Chapter 3 Callback

In this chapter, we discussed ways to spice up your writing. Specifically, we discussed:

- How the simplest structure to a beginning, middle, and end is to: tell them what you're going to tell them, tell them, then tell them what you told them
- How people relate to stories much more than they do numbers or a recitation of facts and how stories are easier for the speaker to remember too
- How to use rhetorical devices—particularly the Power of Three and rhetorical questions—to make your speeches more powerful and memorable
- How repetition is also a strong memory device for your audience
- How the element of surprise keeps your speech lively
- And, how you must cram 50 pounds of potatoes into a five-pound sack and end within your allotted time

Now to close.

And, in Closing …

I've shared some tools with you to make you a better speechwriter. Now it's up to you. There are no shortcuts. Writing, like public speaking, is both an art and a craft. You become better by doing. Join a Toastmasters club and find a mentor who can guide you through your first 10 speeches. Then, once you have your speaking sea legs, find a supportive critic—someone who isn't afraid to tell you the hard truth. I put aside another project I'm working on, a guide to marketing for small businesses, to write this book. I sent a draft of the first chapter of the marketing book to Dr. Stephanie Bluestein, a friend of mine who was once a journalism colleague and is now a journalism professor at a California university. She had many suggestions. But she hit me hard with this advice on a particular outtake:

"If your intention was to aggravate and alienate the entire female population, then you hit the mark. If not, I suggest a revision."

I have been a professional writer for more than 30 years! Do I need this grief?

Yes, I do. Greatness is a journey, not a destination. There are twists and turns, detours, bad weather, bad hair, and accidents along the way. There also are sunny days, smooth roads, and unbelievable beauty. But no shortcuts. If you haven't already, begin your journey to greatness today.

This book was designed to guide you on that journey. Use it, abuse it, and evaluate me by telling me how I can be an even better guide for you. I welcome your feedback.

About the Author

Tom Pfeifer has been a professional communicator for more than 30 years.

For 15 years, Pfeifer was a journalist in Southern California, where he won awards from The Associated Press, United Press International, and others for individual writing and group coverage. During his journalistic career, he stood on a dam in danger of collapsing, landed in a helicopter on a warship rocking in the Pacific Ocean, crawled through a warehouse as aftershocks from the Northridge Earthquake shook the ground violently, walked on petroleum-stained rocks in Alaska's Prince William Sound in the wake of the Exxon Valdez disaster, and witnessed five living presidents dedicate Ronald Reagan's presidential library.

He then moved to the nation's capital to serve as a congressman's press secretary and communications director. There, he communicated his boss's role in the impeachment of President Bill Clinton, the aftermath of 9/11, numerous terrorism hearings, and the release of journalist James Foley from Libya strongman Moammar Ghadafi.

In September 2013, he founded Consistent Voice Communications, LLC, where he serves as Managing Partner and helps small businesses, associations, and individuals Communicate for Success!—through clear, concise, and consistent messaging.

As a congressional communicator, Pfeifer wrote numerous speeches—for other people. But he was too terrified to stand before an audience himself and try to say anything coherent. He joined a Toastmasters club in March 2012, knowing he would have to speak before groups as an entrepreneur. Now he speaks regularly on effective communication techniques. You can reach him at Tom@YourConsistentVoice.com.

Sources

"Attention Span Statistics." Statistic Brain. April 2, 2015. Accessed November 29, 2015. http://www.statisticbrain.com/attention-span-statistics/.

Carlson, Kurt A., and Suzanne B. Shu. "When Three Charms But Four Alarms: Identifying the Optimal Number of Claims in Persuasion Settings." Social Science Research Network. June 11, 2013. Accessed November 29, 2015. http://ssrn.com/abstract=2277117.

Conran, Joshua. "How to Grab Your Target's Attention in 8 Seconds (or Less)." Inc.com. October 13, 2014. Accessed November 29, 2015. http://www.inc.com/joshua-conran/how-to-grab-your-target-s-attention-in-8-seconds-or-less.html.

Dlugan, Andrew. "Spice Up Your Speech writing (Epiphora)." Six Minutes RSS. September 7, 2015. Accessed November 29, 2015. http://sixminutes.dlugan.com/epiphora/#more-6523.

Dlugan, Andrew. "Toastmasters Speech 6: Vocal Variety." Six Minutes RSS. November 1, 2009. Accessed November 29, 2015. http://sixminutes.dlugan.com/toastmasters-speech-6-vocal-variety/.

"Effects of Humor on Sentence Memory." National Center for Biotechnology Information. July 20, 1994. Accessed November 29, 2015. http://www.ncbi.nlm.nih.gov/pubmed/8064254.

"Gestures: Your Body Speaks." Toastmasters International. June 1, 2011. Accessed March 24, 2012. https://www.toastmasters.org/~/media/E202D7AA84E24A758D1BAAE8A77FD496.ashx.

"Inspire Your Audience." In *Competent Communication*, 50. Mission Viejo: Toastmasters International, 2013.

Langello, Kip. "Should You Write for Yourself or for the Reader?" *Writer's Digest*, May 21, 2014. http://www.writersdigest.com/online-editor/should-you-write-for-yourself-or-for-the-reader

"Organizing Your Speech." *The Better Speaker Series.* Toastmasters International. May 1, 2011.

Rotman, Ethan. "How Much Time Do You Really Have To Grab Their Attention?" ISpeakEASY Blog. November 17, 2011. Accessed November 29, 2015. https://ispeakeasyblog.wordpress.com/2011/11/16/how-much-time-do-you-really-have-to-grab-their-attention/.

Stambor, Zak. "How Laughing Leads to Learning." Monitor on Psychology. June 1, 2006. Accessed November 29, 2015. http://www.apa.org/monitor/jun06/learning.aspx.

"Stress Relief from Laughter? It's No Joke." Stress Management. July 23, 2013. Accessed November 18, 2015. http://www.mayoclinic.org/healthy-lifestyle/stress-management/in-depth/stress-relief/art-20044456?reDate=18112015.

Thompson, Jeff. "Is Nonverbal Communication a Numbers Game?" Psychology Today. September 30, 2011. Accessed November 29, 2015. https://www.psychologytoday.com/blog/beyond-words/201109/is-nonverbal-communication-numbers-game.

Trust Is a Must. Performed by Ryan Avery. USA: AveryToday, 2012. Film. https://youtu.be/ReE7-X70iPU

Valentine, Craig. "Call Backs." Lecture, Craig Valentine's 52 Speaking Tips, January 5, 2015.

Valentine, Craig. "Check the VAKS." Lecture, Craig Valentine's 52 Speaking Tips, March 29, 2015.

Valentine, Craig. "3 Keys to Closing your Speech with Great Impact." Lecture, Craig Valentine's 52 Speaking Tips, August 21, 2015.

Appendix: Speech Sample

You Just WAIT Until Your Father Comes Home

[Props: None]

[Stage Center: Kitchen]

"You just WAIT until your father comes home!"

Mr. Contest Master, fellow Toastmasters, and most distinguished guests:

Yeah. I was that kid.

My dad was 6-foot-1. Solid muscle. My mom was 5-foot nothing. Thin as a rail. Everyone knew her for wearing flip flops: weddings, funerals, shoveling snow—flip flops.

But I knew her best for her steely blue eyes—and her wooden spoon. And when her eyes bore into mine and she said those words, chills crawled up my spine.

"You just WAIT until your father comes home!"

[Move to Stage Left: Backyard]

When I was 7, I decided to dig a hole to China. We lived on Long Island in New York and digging into the ground was easy. After about six inches of topsoil, you hit sand—all the way to China. So, I was digging, and digging, and digging. I had dug down about two feet when my mom came out to collect the wash from the wash line, her flip-flops slapping against her heels.

"What are you doing?"

"I'm digging to China, Ma!"

As I turned to look at her, I noticed her clean white sheets had been torn from the line and were buried under a pile of sand. She dropped the laundry basket, grabbed me by the ear and lifted me from the hole.

[Move to Stage Center: Kitchen]

She dragged me into the house, sat me down at the kitchen table, and picked up her wooden spoon.

"You just WAIT until your father gets home."

My dad did come home. My mom led him out to the scene of the crime, her flip flops slapping at her heels. Then they came back into the house. My mom stood across me and laid her wooden spoon on the table. My father said, "Stand up, son." I did, and he put his arm around me.

"We needed a new cesspool, son. Thanks for getting it started. Get out there and keep digging. But watch the laundry!"

[Move to Stage Right: Garage]

When I was 9, my parents decided to add an extension on the house to accommodate my new sister and soon-to-be brother. They stored the shingles for the extension in the garage. The boxes said, "Fire retardant." I decided to find out how retardant. So I slid out the book of matches I always carried in my pocket and struck a match. I put the little flame next to the cardboard box. The little flame turned into a big flame.

[Move to Stage Center: Kitchen]

I ran into the kitchen. "Hi, Mom." I grabbed a glass, filled it with water and [Move to Stage Right: Garage] ran back to the garage. The flames were bigger. [Move to Stage Center: Kitchen] I ran back in, refilled the glass, [Move to Stage Right: Garage] ran back outside, and I could hear my mother's flip flops following me.

"What's going on?"

"There's a fire. I'm putting it out, Ma."

My mom grabbed the garden hose and doused the fire. Then she grabbed me by the ear, [Move to Stage Center: Kitchen] dragged me into the house, sat me down at the kitchen table, and picked up her wooden spoon.

"You just WAIT until your father gets home."

My dad did come home. My mother led him out to the scene of the crime, her flip flops slapping at her heels. Then they came back into the house. My mom stood across me and laid he wooden spoon on the table. My father said, "Stand up, son." I did, and he put his arm around me.

"I knew I shouldn't have put those shingles directly across from a south-facing window. Spontaneous combustion. Thanks for being there to put it out. Want to help me clean it up?"

[Remain Stage Center: Kitchen]

When I was 11, my dad had gotten a ride to work and my mom had left for the store. The keys to my dad's brand new Dodge Dart were sitting on the kitchen table. I picked up the keys. And a phone book. [Move to Stage Right: Driveway] I went out to the car, opened the door, put the phone book on the driver's seat, and climbed in. Even with the phone book I could barely reach the clutch and see over the steering wheel. But I managed to get it started. It stalled at my first attempt. But eventually I got it moving and took it for a spin around the block. All in first gear. As I turned the corner, I saw my mother in the driveway. I pulled the car into the driveway and parked it. Crookedly. Mom said nothing. She simply opened the car door, [Move to Stage Center: Kitchen] grabbed me by the ear, dragged me into the house, sat me down at the kitchen table, and picked up her wooden spoon.

"You just WAIT until your father gets home."

My dad did come home. My mom led him out to the scene of the crime, her flip flops slapping at her heels. Then they came back into the house. My mom stood across me and laid her wooden spoon on the table. My dad didn't say a word. He simply reached across the table, picked up the wooden spoon and handed it to my mom.

There was now a sparkle in those steely blue eyes.

STAND up son, she said.

[Pause]

[Looking up at Dad] Dad?

[Looking at the Contest Master] Mr. Contest Master?

www.ingramcontent.com/pod-product-compliance
Lightning Source LLC
Chambersburg PA
CBHW070108100426

42743CB00012B/2687